DADDY EDGAR'S POOLS

For
Kevin

Best.
Wishes
Mike Hawking

His Singing Bird

Caged in the skull, somedays his gull
Sings of far forgotten seas.
                              At other times a plover,
Sometimes curlew, the sea mew
Supplanted by the high moors' bass.
Night hunting she's an owl
Threading the unfathomed woods by moonwash.
On hot still days a lark spills
From his eyes to carol on the hung
Heights.
Still evenings' quiet a blackbird calls
Beyond the hedger's hook.

All these his singing bird calling uncalled,
Her notes always new,
Clutching in her talons
The quill.

Daddy Edgar's Pools
MIKE HARDING

PETERLOO POETS

First published in 1992
by Peterloo Poets
2 Kelly Gardens, Calstock, Cornwall PL18 9SA, U.K.

Reprinted in 1993

**A catalogue record for this book is available
from the British Library**

ISBN 1-871471-31-1

Printed in Great Britain by
Latimer Trend & Company Ltd, Plymouth

This volume was produced with assistance from
the Ralph Lewis Award at the University of Sussex.

Supported by

LIBRARIES AND ARTS

For Pat
and in memoriam Fr. Augustus 'Foxy' Reynolds,
St. Bede's College, Manchester.

Contents

Photofather

Beside the bowl of stale, puckered fruit
And the cracked jug that holds the rent book,
My teeth and hair and eyes look
Forward from twenty-three years of death,
Begun when parachutes burnt over Holland.
Four weeks later to the day, I wailed my way,
On points, into the all clear Anderson-world,
And began immediately to build from your braid and bible
A pattern of fathers. So I made you out
Of cuttings from the *Eagle* and the *Hotspur* and the *Lion*
And rode you up and down the German-clotted sky
Until you must have been nearly sick to death.
This way I made something, but it was like
A pub piano, alright to vamp for sing-songs
Near the fire by night, but tuneless
And nerve-jangling in the morning's cold: a wax man
Whose wings fell off in the sun.

We rarely talked of you. I could not ask
What you were like, or felt or said—
Bits trickled through the net of pain: your motorbike,
The way you took off Churchill in the train.
They say that I'm your spit and yet we know
The closeness of our common grief would be
Too much. We dust your picture smile and,
Saying nothing, lie.

We have a picture of a cross somewhere
In Holland: a green hump covers up
The bits of you they found. I clutch it still,
Sensing only mystery and loss, and build
You once again each year, cast now
Perennial, in different, stranger moulds.

Daddy Edgar's Pools

Each week you, Thursday Millionaire, would conjure up
The ju-ju, stab the coupon with a pin
Or read the cups, perm my age and height
With Hitler's birthday and the number of
The bus that passed the window and the clump
Of pigeons on the next door neighbour's loft.

With rabbit's foot, white heather, and wishbone
You fluenced the coupon that I ran to post.

Each muggy Saturday you sat still while the set
Called out into the hushed room where I sat
With burning ears and heard a London voice
Call names as strange as shipping forecasts through the air:
Hamilton Academicals, Queen of the South,
Pontefract United, Hearts of Midlothian,
Wolverhampton Wanderers, Arbroath, Hibernian,
And once, I thought, a boy called *Patrick Thistle.*

Then every week after the final check,
When Friday's dreams were scratched out with a squeaky pen,
You took down from upstairs your brass band coat,
Gave me the wad of polish and the button stick.
And there in that still, darkened room I polished up
Each brassy button world that showed my face;
While you on shining tenor horn played out
Your Thursday Millionaire's lament
For a poor man's Saturday gone.

Dust

The way he came in brought a whisper
Of Winter into the summer-warm house.
We saw him so little, my infrequent uncle.
Cement dust bloomed his boots mothpowder soft,

His pants and jacket filmed with white,
His hands hod-cracked, more stone than skin,
In one his dusty plasterer's cap, as though
He'd come to ask forgiveness of the house

Or beg the daughter for a bride.
'I've lost my child', his stone-dry throat clacked in
A song I'd never heard before that was
All wails and chokes and was man-crying.

I saw pictures of Peter Pan, lost boys,
A child crying in a boggart-dark wood,
And he, all dusted like a miller, searching down
The screaming alleys of the witch-black night.

What I could not see, with my seven-year eyes,
Was the baby bending in the street behind
The old greengrocer's van, the faintly-felt
Slow, soft thump, as he reversed,

Of tumbled smallness
Underneath the wheel
That pressed her, like the rolling plum
She sought, into the summer dust.

Dancing on Toes

Round the kitchen on the rag rug
We reeled. Me standing on my mother's toes
Gripping her pinny fast, my nose
Dug in the soft pillow of her belly. Smug

Old Mushy Cat watched from on top
The sewing machine, disdainful, proud.
We turned the volume knob up loud
And danced and danced until the music stopped.

Then, years on years, around I danced
In my mother's kitchen with *my* child balanced
On my toes. Wildly we hopped, higher
We turned the music, and spun turning

And turning, and I looked in the coal fire
And saw suddenly twenty-odd years burning.

Icarus Daedalus

My hero years were spent pasting you into
My life, a blue man taking off, out through
A million moonlit nights. On every one I heard
Lancasters lug their Tall Boys from
Dispersal to the track, marshall, taxi
And lumber out and up, groaning only inches above
The tips of the thunder-shaking wood.

I heard pianos in the wind, and apple fields,
And kiss-red fruit still dancing in the Devon air.
I heard the birds of Lincolnshire call in the dawn
As young men ill with fear made landfall from
The sea of howling night, small boys sat on
Fat cushions piloting the death birds home.

Now, twice your age, I stand where you stood then,
On broken slabs of concrete where bright mats
Of 'airfield weed' are moving in. The tangled
Closeting woods make this dispersal point a grove,
Still place of birds, and nothing changes but that you,
A ghost, walked here my Icarus, my Daedalus,
My father now my son. I wish that I could say
Some words to this still air, but they would be lost
In the small birds' innocent mockery.
I take a clump of stonecrop for the rockery.

Mushycat

Had a cat, Mushycat,
Old before I was born,
Lived greyly another ten years after that,
A bony cushion cuffed off chairs.

Scruffy cat,
Dawdled on rooftops rimed by the frosty moon,
Rubbed about the chimbleys with his whiskers cocked
And, like a black knight,
Mated and went his way.

Lame cat,
Lost eight of his nine lives
Fighting coal carts, buses and whippets,
And disappeared to lose the ninth
One Christmas Day.
Found him,

Mushycat,
Stiff cat, a starched muff,
Cardboard-model, bogus cat,
Not our cat, flesh and fur cat, hob corner cat,
Steal the meat cat, trip my gran cat.

But it was him cat;
Scarred nose from Corkett's dog,
Ear ripped in a tomfight,
Tail kinked in a careless kitchen door,
Legs all crooked and gangly,
And the fur half on, half off.

Dead Cat,
Our cat, Mushycat,
Lay, wide-eyed and grinning at death,
The hero-warrior of my tenth year,
Stiff as a full stocking in the Christmas snow.

What Did You Learn in School Today?

Today, as well as the names of Britain's major ports,
And the names and tonnage of her exports,
And how Thomas à Beckett died, and how cocoa is made,
I learnt that the poor stink.
Today at eight years and three quarters
I learnt that they smell of stale, close rooms,
Of bad teeth, bleeding gums, and unwashed clothes;
That they smell of tenements where
Dark, drunk men piss on stairways
And couples fuck in the rubbish chute,
While above, dull lights shine through uncurtained glass.
Today I learnt how the poor smell of bad food and sour milk.
And how they stink of sleeping
Seven to a bed, how their mothers are born old and tired
And how their fathers burn their eyes out at the fire,
Staring and workless, looking for hope in the dying coals.
I learnt how they live by rivers purple with dye
And scummed with rats, how they fear the Saturday night
With its beery breath and brawling, bawling fights
And noisy babygetting on the lurching, shrieking bed
In shaking houses near the shunting yards.

I learnt all that in school today:
That and the names of all our kings and queens
In order.

Sparrowfart

He called it at the paper shop that smelt of newsprint,
Fags and chocolates, and hot sweet tea.
This paperboy had been up three hours already.
Up and out and wild-eyed at the dawn's coming,
Watching him rub the grey out of the eyes
Of the world, kicking the sandman's arse for him.
No breakfast, I cranked my old bike out
Through streets where timid birds just dared
A morning cough before the chimneys' smoke.

That Summer's dawn I went for miles
Through ghost-town suburbs to the edge where red-
Brick foundered on old barns, pig-sties and ponds.
Dew-burnished moors burnt in a rising lemon light
That was stronger than a prayer, and air so fine it sang
Ran over hills where pinched stone farms
Were waking to the first warm slats of light,
Cows moaning, cocks gabbling, and the crags
All spattered with foam-flecks of sheep. I stood
Agog with all the web of walls, the crisp crags
And the purpled moors climbing to meet
The small white hustlers of cloud at the world's rim.

Then I biked back towards the town and work,
As waking streets grumbled over toast and lost
Fag-packets, and school bus fares. And I rammed
The *Guardians, Sketches, Heralds* and the *Mirrors* through
The doors—Sparrowfart. I finished, rode to school,
The moors and miles still shining in my eyes, and answered
'Present', though I wasn't. I was out there still,
Not in this dull, chalky room in the city heat. I was
Stood still on the moor's bright border,
My feet on millstone grit, while sun and wind
Raddled the heather, and I drank the wine of the day.

Old Man Farrer

Old Man Farrer spat gaptoothed on you when he talked,
Booted his pigs in the belly to move them, walked
The length of the village once pulling a ringed boar
By his little finger, knew more

About pigs and dug more graves in a day than any man
Around. He cradled birth-wet steaming piglets in hands
Like fleshy shovels and had been, they said,
Man for any woman once in hedge, field or bed.

A funeral done, he boozed down in *The Waterloo*
And once he told us how he buried his Jews
Stood up in plywood coffins on Bungs Hill.
There the dyeworks and the railway had crept up until

Less than a tenth of his land was left.
Now the chickens, pigs, old vans and derelict barns were adrift
Somehow, a scattering of lean-tos looking down
On the graves, the dyeworks, the triumphant town

Clutched damp and smouldering in the valley.
Through the graveyard on autumn-foggy
Dawns, his sooty pigs wandered amongst marble
Tombs snuffling, rooting in the monumental gravel.

And Old Man Farrer followed in the fog, terrible
Swineherd, bawling and shouting with the smell of swill
And tobacco, pigshit, gravedamp, and beer flowering
And blooming as he lurched along booming

By the tracks and steam pipes hissing overhead,
Piloting pigs over the town and long-lying dead.

It Has Snowed Leaves All Day

It has snowed leaves all day; last night
First-frost snapped stalks, and now the road
Is lime-white, coated in the lamplight
With their matted, brittle curls.

The cars have ploughed a pathway through
The drifts, and singing children come
Cob-coaling, kick spindrift beneath
The street lamp's bitter, yellow light.

Tomorrow the air will be ripe
With the smell of burning snow.

Hack

Mark him well, the ash on his collar,
The mints he sucks to cover the booze
On his breath,the slightly scuffed shoes,
One hand in the fingerbowl. For thirty dollars

He'll filch from the mantlepiece
The killer's wedding photograph;
Knows who had sex with a psychopath,
Knows a chat-show host who's screwing his niece.

He'll camp in his fag-fugged car all night
Outside your house:
Go through your bins, get under your skin, tight
As any crab louse.

His shaking fingers on the keys
Blister souls, suck like hagfish,
And there's no use shouting back because he
Has the last word. The dot matrix

Wielded by this goading prick,
Is always mightier than the sword.

Old Pro

His fan-pic hangs in many a dining room,
Above the sideboard where landladies keep
The brown sauce and the cornflakes and the bread.
Theatrical boarding house. The legend scrawled
Proclaims 'Good Luck. To Flo. Smashing Digs.'

He lies. He made an act around the food,
And three or four bad gags from her stinking sheets.
She remembers him with pride. He was second top.
He took their Maureen in her pram down to the park
Between the tubeworks and the yards, a proper nice
Quiet man, but such a card, always a laugh.

He dies now nightly in bad run-down clubs;
Suffers the jeers, the boozy women with permed hair
And red slashed mouths, the men who look
Thinking 'Poor bastard what a way to end'.
Suffers the youths who spew before the stage
And the treasurer's begrudging paying-off,
The promise 'Have you back' that never comes.
Stuffs beer-soaked notes into his wallet and
Walks out, his collar folded up, hearing
The rain's unscripted patter on the bins.

Birmingham, Scunthorpe, Hartlepool, Crewe, Stoke,
Rotherham, Walsall, Battersea: his life
Reads like a railway almanac. Those days
He took the Sunday train with other pros
To start a weekly run. Winter—panto:
The laughing kids, the bangs, costumes, and lights;
The frontline girl who thought it worth her while
To go down between shows for the second top.
Summer—the seaside piers, the mud and sea,
The sands-end, arse-end town, digs near the docks.
The easy girls on Wakes weeks from the mills,

Legs spread apart beneath the strutting pier
As the night sea licked the salt-scabbed iron piles
And the sea breeze and his stage-croak whispered 'love'.
A bag of chips, a quick punch up the drawers,
He became the postcard life of his own gags.

Now he cracks out his life in beery halls
And meets occasionally in hotel bars
Another pro like him 'doing all right',
'Waiting for some news', 'A telly bit', 'A cruise'.
They never come. Night after night he waits
Till the loud group have ripped off their last chord
Then he struts on to silence and blank stares.
Wearing his patter like a coat, his timing gone,
He sweats and dies the death. When morning comes
He rings his agent: 'Went a bomb last night'.
Both know he lies. His agent will keep him on
Until he's worked him out. And then he'll be
Alone until the final catcall comes
And he hangs up his parts and props and suits
And pastes himself into the last page of
His scrapbook.

Flute Player

for Phil Sloyan, Co. Mayo and Manchester

As down the glen came McAlpine's men
Their shovels slung behind them,
It was in the pub that they supped their sub
And it's down in the spike you'll find them.

Chopped fingers flickering on the keys,
Span out the smoky room and keen
A music made forgotten years ago
A teem of times in houses in the West.
By lurking peat you learned the tips and cuts,
And trod dark country miles to fill
The reeking harvest barns with tunes
Till the room grew quiet again;
And in the dawn your slow airs lured
The birds down from the trees and called
The lovers from the roadside ditch.
Here now the room is brassy with
The smell of work, and brick-faced men
With hands like hods breathe malty barside
Talk of homes they'll see no more. While through
It all, your eyes tight-closed, your bald
Head slightly, tenderly bowed, the old
Airs warm the room: *Boy in the Gap,*
Tenpenny Bit, and *Banish Misfortune.*
And the bar-room moves as an old man,
Lopsided with his stout, trips neatly,
Lightly, through the measure of a jig
He last heard at a cross-roads in the West.
They little know, those Saxons on the site
That a poet and a piper walk their midst.

Tomorrow those same fingers rule a line
Or flick curled shavings from a new-planed length,
Feed bright brass screws into the yielding grain,
As the lilting of the diesel fills the air.

Riches

Bungalows, Toyotas on the bog,
Code signifiers of
A new colonial lexicon.
Within a screen flickers and the game show dances
For empty gumboots drying by the stove,
As the brand new Subaru trails sucklers
To the mart along a Euro road.
So a soft day sweeps veils of rain
Over the Blasketts and trails them
Along the Kerry hills, melting them into glens
To wash down gullies into Anascaul.

The colour TVs glow above shag-pile, outside
White porticos and columns, breeze-block castles,
Lions rampant, eagles over the milk churns,
And The Gates of Glory that Fionn marched through
In triumph is now lassooed
By a concrete garden wall,
A smart new gravelled drive.
Fionn's white strand
Where the Fianna vanquished the King of the World
Some British sapper turns to Ventry.
Some gombeen developer with a soul bypass
Wants to turn to time-share, leisure-centre,
Theme-park, rainbow's end, fools gold.
New bogus roads zag up the glen and fresh
Barbed wire declares a mountain owned.
And so the coach loads come, the tours,
The Blarney Buses, Darby O'Gulled to see
The new 'interpretative centres' with their audio-
Visual display, toilets, tea and gifts—Real Irish
Peat-work statues—Trace your family name—
Real Leprachauns—Real Shellalaghs—
Real Shamrock Tea Towels—Real Fun!

Below, sunk deep, the tough bog-oak of words,
Oghams, nuggets, nodes

Pulsing under the peat, lode
And ore, word and lore.
Still poor men's diamonds, veins of tongue run on,
Soft clusters of aspirates, the poised rise,
The cadenced fall.
On Croughmarhin the tiger's eye of poetry,
And in An Droighead Beog
Blinding in their bright profusion,
Riotous showers, gems of notes
Pouring from the snotter of a flute.

Kells Scribe

I with gall and goose in cold cell kept
My tryst with spiders; and with vellum,
Sand, and gold-leaf beat breath-thin.

In drudgery I made a pyramid of His words.
I no name have and my brittle quill of bones
In earth has written its last verse,
Fecit Est.

In the Archaeology of the Heart

We delve for spirits and for souls,
Brushing away the filaments of years,
Scraping, seeking the lintel of the crypt,
Unwinding cerements, decanting vials,

Smoothing the nub of bone. The catacombs
Ring to our chatter as we search the rooms.
The faces of our dead are printed in
The dust, a breath on a mirror films,

Then draws off. We finger scripts in the silt,
Mouth words, gauging the half-life of our lust,
The palimpsest of love, shards of joy,
Urn-burials of pain, torcs of finest guilt.

And still lacunae, glyphs, fall from the wall;
Old ghosts are howling at the moon.

Cliffs of Moher

Shrunk suddenly to the size of gull-droppings
You finger the edge and look down
At sea clowns on Goat Island, and
Hung skeins of air where fulmars wheel and skit,
Split nibs in the currents of air below,
Exploring planes and sliding through dimensions,
Slotting at the cusp of an arc into stasis,
Then riding the updraught down.

Waves that left America roll up the base
Of these hung tapestries of stone,
Voices from the coffin-ships mutter
And thunder at their base
Beating the drums of under-sea jungles.
Below your belly, as you lie,
The snakes are curled in the slab,
Worms that shuddered here when this edge
Of the world was mud, and half the world asleep.

A sense of fear, of awe, of longing draws you,
Sucks you to the edge where, a wingless Daedalus,
You stand, the waves gulling you to jump
And leave a scream like a rip in the air.

Thomas Fisher

1.
Only the abbot's fish-monk,
Net hauler, net caster, fisher of fish
Not men, tugging sunk
Bombs of carp from the peat-dark ponds,
Gold nuggets squirming through time:
Finny roach, spiny perch, and
Abbot-plump bream too soft-gobbed to hook.
Only a poor slap-pate monk;
One tooth, crook foot, back twisted like an angry fist.

2.
'Chuck 'en on the midden!'
'Wait', said Old Biddy, 'Yet there's life in it!'
Sap in a twisted briar!'
She upped me and slapped me arse.
I cawed and the ice crackled on the fish ponds.

Seventy years ago, and for sixty
On 'em I've watched the moon's slow
Waltz over the rhines,
The withy's nobbled heads
Wearing her like a halo.
Voice too cracked for plainsong,
Hands too swolled for the quill, I pulled,
Peter-like, the sweet
Mirror-skinned darlings from the deep.
Old Thomas.

The young monks went skip 'tulla lulla' by,
I shuffled skewshanked with my basket.
'Old Thomas, they'll be stinking
By the time they swim in the pot.'
Bede the baker gave me bread,
Brass-bellied carp came up to kiss

Loudly the roof of their world, bussing, smacking,
Sucking at the coat-tails of infinity;
As I, like God himself, threw manna from on high,
Alms to the supplicants of the deep.

3.
Lowest of the lowly I lived out on the moss,
Bones sodden as old sunk logs, bog-oak, water-clogged.
Pains rang through as first frosts came and iced the marrow;
Knuckles like tubers, arms hooped in with cramp.

But worms live through the wildest storm,
Delve deeper in the hottest drought,
And only I am left. The slow worm sneaks
Under the sentry's boot.

4.
When Hal's men took the abbot and his monks,
They left Old Tom, that hook-backed, fish-wife's clout.
So I stood by the fishponds in the summer's heat
And saw him passing on the hurdle gibbering,
His Confiteor Dei gabbled by the hurdle's 'ran tan tan';
His rich cloths torn away, all shite-besmirched, his fat
Slack, fish-white belly wobbling to
The cobbles' paradiddles. No King's man,

God's man in spite of all their 'stolen chalices'.
He, hanged, sings Mass now to the crows, black acolytes
Bowing and clacking out their offertory.
They circle still, I hear their Dies Irae round
By Joseph's Thorn. They're singing of the years
To come, the stained glass fallen in the dust, the gouts
Of red from Herod's cloak, the Ark and Noah's blue
Sea all in splinters, and the shining Virgin's face
Crunched under soldiers' boots.

The old dispensation changes,
The world has come to the market place
And the butchers dance in the shambles.
It is a time for quiet hunchbacks.

July Barbers

From Mayo, God help us, each summer they came
And stood to be hired in Salt Kettle Lane
And the farmers would pass with a swagger and a nod,
A hand slap, a wink, the chink of a few bob,
To drink 'your man's health' and the bargain was struck—
Binding them to the land.

                       The truck
Picked them up when the pubs had all shut
And tipped them, drunk and staggering,
Into the lamplit yard, their beery breath
Wreathing round the moth-danced flame.

                Then it was weeks of
Scything, raking, turning, loading,
Sun-up to the edge of light
When blood spilled, ran, and filled the sky,
And men grew field-long stalking shadows.
Sleeping an hour they rose, swilling the night
Out of their eyes at the trough, washing
The gall of loneliness from their mouths,
The smell of bacon fingering the air
As mist smudged a heron on the river and a curlew
Bubbled at the orange ball that rimmed the fell.
Sunday, sixteen miles to mass, on foot,
And sixteen back, then a few pints and the crack,
Three hours of bed and another rising—'God bless the work!'

Some nights they sang in Irish beneath a shaking moon,
Moving through the watery light
Over a land fecund with seed and fruit.
They combed the hayfield mowing to the lilt
Of an old song and called God's blessing on
The field's pan-scrub chin, well razored.
'Tis a shave will last all year mister!'

Later, from the barn the farmer heard
The soft murmur of Gaelic chanting,
'Like bloody Ju-Ju it sounded, Methody ranting.'
Peering through a crack he saw them kneel
Circled in the lamplight, as horny fingers,
Scythe-segged, told the Rosary through
And Pen-y-Ghent became Crough Patrick.

Trees

There were trees once
Thick spread across this moor
Until monks, scuttling brown
Slugs, crossed the forest floor,

And staggering through the naves
Of that green abbey
Under the axes' weight,
Gave a few smart snickering blows
And dissolved a clerestory of leaves
In a muttering of thunder heard across the dale.

Now blocks of spruce
In regimented rows march up the fell.
Their hollow halls are barren, no birds sing.
Their needles—you might say—are functional.
Like a modern church, there are no corners here,
No bloodstains on the stone, no devil's footprints,
No gargoyles, no green men, no history, no myth;
Just a London pension fund
At prayer, electric fence all round
A concentration camp for trees.

Now across the fell's bare shoulder
Deer scud from ghyll to ghyll
Searching for the priest holes
Of the relict wood.

Earth

Through the eye socket of the skull
A solitary thistle-speared space,
What was left of the rest of the yowe
Huddled under the hag, bones softening in the rain
Melting back into the land.

Clay-bound he clambers up the fell
To check his fence, knows every sheep full well
By face, and knows her lambs. Knows which one will
Be where, hiding out, lurking, looking for the gap
To get her back into the meadow's hay.

Between earth and sky he is minister
To an ungodly congregation whose creed is grass,
Whose devils wind and rain, snow and maggots.

The land has him in its claws, took him as a child
And is slowly bending him, hazel-hooped.
They have a word about here: *heughed*,
Said like 'he oofed', it means the way
That sheep bind to their little patch of fell.
God knows I never knew that men could *heugh* as well.

Now Along

Now along the dale's rim an owl
Gathers darkness to herself, with breath-soft wings
Pressing the shadows around the out-field barn
Where shrew and vole are rigid at her passing.

Over Rise Hill the old moon grows:
A slow, slick, silver, lime-white slug
Curving its back, and rounding to
A pod, bubbling on the crag's lip,
Then taking to the sky, a bright
Round coin to snug in the ferryman's palm.

Now while the dale is asleep
The night watchers move on the margin of light,
Always edged, on the curve,
Coming and going, sidereal.

A walker halts by a peat-black pool, his dog
Snuffles among leaves, paws a log.
Looking in the pool, it is hard
To see which is the froth and which the stars.

Searching for Lambs

Was filling your lungs with glass,
Rodding the Christmas card world; Lass
Sniffing, yowling, biting the suddenly soft-bleached field.
Under the fell the brunt of snow has fallen,
Under the crag the flood rides swollen; frozen
Wind-blown Hokusai waves, house-deep.
A fathom down the lambs are breathing slowly,
Wondering at the dream they are becoming.

Those he digs out are drunk, mazed
In the sudden warmth of his leather hands;
Are lapped in sacks to coddle by the stove
In a kitchen loud with spinning, clutching children.
The missing slowly drown, becoming woollen boomerangs,
Appearing only when the thaw draws back again
The slow pale curtain of this bogus Spring.

Molecatcher

They lie strung on the wire drying in the sun.
A leather rosary atop the lane-end wall,
A decade-and-a-half of mowdies tell the light
They once were dark and grubbed the peaty soil.
His eyes seek out the shovellers, look for signs.
As they torpedo on, he marks them by
Their heaves, gauges their runs. Ten Acre field
Is cleared and River Flatts, the peaty boils
Are lanced and set with steel, marked with a stick
And left to do their work. He does his rounds
Next day and sees with simple pride the sprung
Traps, hooks them out and hangs them on the wire.

They die within two hours, trapped in the seams
They know so well. He digs them up before
They stink and spoil his snares. Out in the light
You'd hardly think they'd warrant all this care,
This killing. Each small body turns head down,
Claws splayed out, still swimming in the light.
The yet-warm, fur-slug sack of blood and bone
That bombed through peaty fields, undercut stone,
Swings slow and dries out in the moorland wind.
They tell the farmer Harry's work is done,
And as they turn and rot and baffle crows
They work again and earn a pint or two
And smokes when back-end reckoning comes around.

Hillfarmer

A hump of hay slung high across his back,
Thorn-bole fingers clutching the baling twine's
Slack. Ask him a question and the cracked
Lips, a wound in a field of silver stubble, in time

Will open and measured words placed
Like stones on drystone walls will add up, through
And cripple-hole and stile. He laces
Words together, handles them with journeyman care, like tools.

His teeth are stumps, half-cock sarsen on
The ridge of his gums, and his eyes
Lie back in the sockets of his skull, dun
Twin foxes in their dens. The night

Frost sculpts his breath in my door light.
We talk of the weather, last week's snow,
The coming thaw, lambs right
To drop. He turns to go,

We nod goodnight. He hucks his load
And up the hill he lumbers through the dark
To his bare land clutched and bowed
In the Combe's bay, withered, stark.

Each haytime he rakes footcocks by moonlight:
Down Dale they tractor big bales under lamps.
With rabbit, badger, falcon, mole, and shrike
For neighbours, he sits over the fire. Cramps

Wrack him, rain nails him to the fell,
Rams him in there like a fist.
Boxed in by the crags his last years well,
Lap at him like a rising mist.

The long-case clock ticks softly in the hall
While round his house owls of the future call.

An Old Dalesman Foresees his Death

To have gathered in the faggots, dragged them up lanes
Clagged with late summer mud
In a wind that tugs the sheep-lugs
Off the wire, and a slashing rain

That rattles the old shed's grimy pane;
To have them soldiered and stood, stiff,
In pensioned pride, still grappling with
The subtle illusion of a job well done,

Seems all to the good as they lie piled
Along the bad loose-litter, recked
Against Winter and her hoar's breath, when the rind
And rime of frost will curd the mist-hung beck.

Till I think on I may not live to see
The green ash tremble into ember, crack
And split, and flames curl around the fireback.
When the house is ragged by the gales of February

And the ice-furred lane fades in the mustering dark,
Some other hands will warm at my hands' work.

Drystone Waller

In memoriam Tom Morphet—Horton in Ribblesdale, Settle, Yorks.

Curling horned fingers in an ancient craft
First learnt when tribes fleshed forts on Simon Fell,
Old Tom finds chink and cheek of stone and lays
And beds them jowl and root, not pausing till
Lined up to his frame, stone after stone grows, packs
And fits with through and capstone, the fell, bare
Bones of these wind-scoured dales. Here fields are made
From nowt and nourished, and a gap can loose
A flock or lease a bull sprung lurching on
A neighbour's cow. Old Tom, the waller, works
His craft, keeps Time and warrior winds at bay
While up the fell the walls cross bogs, skirt pots,
And lie along the tops to patch the land.
'A gap is down' means hours of hard, rough, hand-
Work, tearing skin on stone, bare footings, chip
Fillings, slabbed stile and cripple hole. He shakes
His head at bedsteads in a gap and rough-
Piled walls, a scrimshank farmer's art. But when
They want a real wall, then they send for Tom
Who'll stand in weather-how and work all day
And make a wall to stand a hundred years
To piece again the pattern of the dale.

Falcons

Fisted on the ledge they suddenly flex
And caress the air, he first, she next;
And, scythe-like, lie on the murmuring rise
As though on another, solid dimension.
Surface tension holds them slowly, riding the liquid.

Below farms are shrunk to slots
And tracings, sheep grubs, cows ants.
I, belly-down on crag's edge, follow their
Orbit, the trajectory of their majesty.

Hung bombs, they kill on the wing,
Wind-arrows dropping from infinity
On wood-dove, and racing-pigeon. Their
Nest an underwood of pink-scaled legs:
Three chicks, grenades of down amongst shell shards
And a mound of numbered alloy rings.

In a sudden swoop they explore the dale's far flanks.
They bank and parabola above Helms Gill
And Rottenbutts; a wide arc brings them back
Their screeches' counterpoint.
Then silent they hang,
Turning widdershins in state; galleons, riding
The rolling of a gentle swell. And then they see the kill.
A sudden bunching; he stoops, a hurtling rock
Erasing a pigeon from the currents below.
She screams, in mid-flight, arc to swooning arc.
He passes her the broken dove,
While through the troubled eddies of the air
A single feather seesaws to the canopied wood.

I marvel at the mastery of it all as
Clenched on the ledge she begins the butchery.
Her hooked bill rives sinew, plucks meat;
Chicks shuffle, dance and mew, sensing blood.

Then, a sudden jet cresting Rise Hill rips the air,
Dips a wing, banks, and turns down dale
So close I see his face—and suddenly
Know how the homing pigeon feels.

Stoneman

It's not hard to guess how griped
And sour you'd become stacked and stitched-
Up in these bare moorland parishes;
Squeezing your life's breath from the stone,
Seeing the clouds corrupt the crops
At the fell's edge, counting the dead
Lambs every spring and watching a calf
Go blind in hours, its eyes two globes of milk
Staring at the boskin slate.

He's weathered it now for nearly seventy years,
Seen land bubble, boil and burst after
Weeks of rain and a whole field toboggan
Down the fellside into the river
Carrying walls and folds before it.

Seen hay lie out in weeks of grey, sour rain
To brown and rot, a year's grass gone to slime
In days. He's seen ice unlock stone,
and frozen hares stood looking into a world
Of nowt, their last breath riming their whiskers.
He's seen winters when an ocean of snow
Has run ashore and paused in waves
House-high. He's cut a tunnel through
To cross from shippon to peat house
And travelled that white catacomb for weeks.

Now he's fisted as tight as a stump
In a thorn hedge. Gripped like a rock
In a root. He sits on his cold flags
Burning a lump of coal at a time.
A packet of tea lasts a month, the stone
Walls of his house sweat with damp, and
On his bare board table, by oil-lamp light,
He scrapes the mould from off the bread,
And in the silent chapel of his mind
Only the wind roars.

He owns five farms now, a pool winner's bounty,
But, as the stone slates of his house
Smart under hail, he patrols alone
His tumbling acres. Coughs cramp him as,
An old sack caping his shoulders,
He trudges through the storm counting his stock,
Hoarding his bare mountain next to his skin.
He wouldn't part, they say, with the steam
From his own piss. Now he holds fast the sour land
In an old tin trunk below his fusty bed.

On the far fell-edge the warrior cairns
Salute him; stone men standing where the mountain's bones
Outcrop. When he dies then stone will mark
Him down—just such and such a man.
They'll come and read—'he lived, he died',
Just so.
        Once crawled upon, now lies below,
The stone.

In Swaledale

In Swaledale Lal Tommy Woof sits up:
A lone cow calving in the byre's his charge.
She nuzzles the stall and Tommy fills his cup
From the flask. Above the Corpse Way and the yard

A hard moon rubs the margin of the dale,
Troubled by rain-coming clouds.
A yowe stands, graven on the river's edge.
A bat, a sudden slash in the air, sails out,

Orbits the barn once and is gone. From a ledge,
As a light rain starts to fall, hunting owls call.

In Dentdale lovers lie below the bridge. Legs
Twined they rock, soft cries and softer calls.
A tawny owl, sweet as a moth, slides overhead,
Sees the pale flesh, hears the murmurs fall.

In Ribblesdale a signal-man talks down the line
To Settle: horse names, odds, times,
Some radio news from Russia, family, friends—
A celebration of the ways and days of men.

And over all of this: Lal Tommy's barn,
The signal-box, the lovers beneath the bridge;
Softer than the dust from any moth's wing,
Softer than the skin of any shaky-new calf,

Softer than any lover's wet-mouthed after-kiss
The soft rain from Chernobyl falls.

Fungi

These slow pods blown from the sod's sponge
Are sour stars sprung upon the darkness of the moss.
Their sweet stink lies on the breath of wind
That tugs the sheep-lugs on the wire,
And whispers rumour in the trees.

These ivory cankers, tumours on the bog,
Are subtle netsuke, moonstone cabochons,
Clustered growths, gravepearls.
All they need to prosper is damp, death, and rot.

On the moor's belly the domes squat:
Drones, their tendrils turning, delicately fingering
The pulse of air. From their guts we hear
The scanner's constant gyre and groan.
Their nerve cells translate the twitterings of space,
The stars' gossip into menace, moves, and threats.
Nervous, they hear zombies in the gorse,
But it is only twitching to the wind's morse.

A rosary of homecoming geese sets the domes shaking,
The screens gibbering, diodes going supernova.

Their spores if they burst
Will transmute the world.

Moors Murders

I'll never compass it: thought wanders, sunk, defeated,
Struggling to see sense in a ritual like this—
This Tollund-like dismissal—children, bas-relief in peat.
The moors have a meaning of their own, they exist

Like the desert to humble. The slashed hags
Are wounds upon the moor, the moss a world agog
With water. Eveywhere streams mutter, land sucks, mind snags
On heather clumps, stumbles, gripped by quaking bog.

So the moors' enormity, and the sense that what happened here,
Has much to do with the twilight of the soul,
Touches on the trackways into Hell. The wind jeers,
Sniggers. In its clutch the tape-recorded screams are rolled

Like prayer-wheels crying for an answer. And this,
And the silver images of babies, broken and twisted,
Leads me across the moor to the edge of the abyss.
Our common cause should lead us to some bridge:

It doesn't. I look down the peat pits and I smell
Sour murder. The cotton-grass shakes a dull fist,
And I see again a father in despair still
Running by night across streets slick with mist,

His child's school photo in his hand. What terrible, dark God
Would call for such a sacrifice as this?
Such acolytes in such a tawdry room? The bog
Shakes in fever. The mind stumbles on words like Auschwitz,

Belsen, Hiroshima, and sees the Apocalypse
In a council house, the spattered walls:
Armageddon in the hands of clerks. In a black pool, lit
By the dying day, I see a sudden figure. It is myself, that's all:

A huddled man-shape, Neanderthal, distrustful, afraid, cold;
Creating phantoms on the innocent moor. The bog holds
Those pathetic, butchered children in her womb, folds
Them to her, votive to the darkness of the soul.

I look down at my hands in the gathering dark
And see only the inky fingers of a clerk.

Drowned Cities

Semerwater drown, Semerwater sink
That never gave nor meat nor drink.

Then it was just one angel turned away,
Limping, fast-fisted to the hills,
Cursing the spire and smoking forge
To submarine and fish-ministered stasis.
Through streets, by shops and inns,
Eels inch, and patrolling pike
Lunge from their dens high amongst gargoyles.
Caddis grub burrow in roof tiles,
And chubb and bream mouth the moss
That furs the flooded ingle.
In the forge's cave an old slow giant roach
Nuzzles at the slime-filled hearth.
Carp loom through bell towers,
Mouthing lichen on dull clappers.
Men, walling on far fells, hear them out-ring,
Swung, by the lake's slow undertow tugged.
The light in flakes and crescents flicks
On chapel walls and rotting pews
Where hymns of pride and glory sounded once,
And crayfish kneel in the craw-thumper's stall.

Now we turn no angel but the world
Away, and children in the Horn of Africa
Are eyes and leather bags.
In cities, men and women lie, chilled meat
In cardboard, deep-freeze dormitories.
Rain forests fall and lakes catch fire,
Berg-birth-grounds thaw, the world's skin falls to rags,
Blood spatters the rowan a month before its time,
A hole the size of Asia in the sky.
A whiff of Aushwitz blows along the Baltic,
And the rain is tinted with plutonium's kiss.

Listen, and above the cities' Karaoke,
The juke box and the game show, and the ranting
Politicians' cant, the stock jobber's dribble, you can hear
It, just—a breathy, whispered rumour in the wind.
                                        Just listen now,
And pray to the God of little fishes when you hear
The lap of rising waters at the dwindling shore.

A Dream of Mermaids

Becalmed, we rode the swell of slow dog days
That sulky pawed the hag's tit canvas;
The slick sea, oily, brass-faced, big-bosomed,
Would bloat and fall, leaden, to Old Neptune's snore.
Our still ship rooted, stuck in his slack belly,
A wedge of living souls, rolled
With this limp and languid, tilting world.

We put out boats and rowed, towing,
And whistling for a wind, with frigate birds
Nib scratches on the sky. The shanty man
His voice a blank, his throat a husk, his lips
Like ripped sea boots, grew laggard, got death drunk,
Fell overboard one night, now sings to squid
And shark his forebitters and capstan rounds.
The armourer went mad and drank hot lead
For musket balls to slake his thirst. The sailmaker
Now counts his canvas, spans it out in shrouds.

One hot night, slipping round the keel they came,
Calling, their voices sweet as the cool breeze
Spun off a Cornish cliff. Men clotted at the rails
And dreamed of homes, lanes glassy in the morning air,
And children's hands holding, following homegoing feet.
Then moonlight shook on the water in flakes and blades
And they were gone, their jagged laughter
Mocking silver bubbles spiralling from the deeps.
Dawn came, a smear on the empty horizon,
Gun-metal-heavy, the sky lying on us sweet as a corpse,
But with it, just the thinnest rumour of a wind,
A door somewhere opening,
A tree somewhere shivering, and
White horses rolling up a Devon shore.

Green

Limp, in a tunnel buttressed by the tongues
And transepts of coiled ferns, while picking berries, he
Lies back and melts and lets the swelter of the summer
Lie on him soft and moist, a young girl's mouth.
Heat washes in whorls memories of innocence,
Childhood, and other tunnels green as this.

An undertidal current stirs the green
Fan-coral at the bottom of this sun-
Striped sea. Bee fishes swim from shell
To shell, the yellow, brittle clusters, clots
Of flowers. The waves of sea-warm breezes wash
This vegetable world. Climbing further back he coils,
A foetus limp in the womb of the green sea-cave,
Its wall studded with pearls of blood and jet.

The voices of his children calling him
Become his mother and he hides amongst
Coiled shells, smells a fermenting world. Fathomed
He founders, washed by the green summer seas
In this autoclave, a brew of fern and fog,
While above a foam of pollen-dusty heads
Washes towards the distant trembling coast.

His coat a bright buoy flapping on
The fence leads mermaid-silkie children down
Through currents of green foam flecked with cerise
Down to this cave to find this Green Man
Truant by the hedge, his face flecked with viridian light,
And laughing, they take him by the sleeve
To drag him drowning back to land.

The Secret Life of Stone

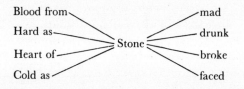

Blood from — Stone — mad
Hard as — Stone — drunk
Heart of — Stone — broke
Cold as — Stone — faced

Slandered and condemned,
The words judge us to death.

But see how water flows from our groins,
How we rim the moor's edge
And dandle climbers from our lips.

See how we take the acid rain and sweeten it,
Cup it, and send it shivering and twitching
In soft veils falling to the valley floor.

See how we, the skeleton of the world,
Stand in circles singing and
Our carved heads grin through eternity.

See how kings have made us cloaks
And stood us, castled on the hill,
To scorn the bent-back peasants at their work.

But words are not our enemies, just time,
And wind and rain, sun and frost.
See how we melt and pucker and fold
When the weasel water gnaws into our bones,
And the maggot ice nibbles us.

Blown and rubbed, the Bridestones fall,
The forts and palaces crumble as the beaches rise,
And stone, from moor to estuary,
Takes to the wind, feathered motes,
Reeling dust, stone dancing.

Stone Mason—Green Man

Beeswax soft, stroke on stroke builds clustered curls.
Eyes blink and the serpent begins to furl,
Devour its tail, giving a lie to the line of Time:
The end is also the beginning,
I am He that is old serpent, devil god,
Time, the *Thief of the World.*

The chisel nibbles the grain,
Dust fumes and feathers the air.
With snicking tip and pecking mell
He coaxes out worms, coiled hair.
A head bites snaking branches,
A stone-chat echoes the chisel's chirps.
A curlew calls, a chisel rip in the sky.
The stone rings, sings, breathes,
And the man holds back the mallet, abashed
At what through him is fathered forth.

Wetpatch

And afterwards, the blackbird in the thorn
Still echoing our slowly-quietening hearts,
You got up to make some coffee and I turned,
Seeing the small, damp ellipse printed on
The sheet, a moist oval, a cabochon
Slit by a darker hair-line, just as though
Upon the linen we had both bestowed
A kiss.

Row One: Morning Becomes Electric—a Synopsis

ACT ONE

Scene 1

The curtains open on their very ordinary life
And Mr and Mrs Lear batter each other with home-truths.

Scene 2

They push in the knife of innuendo,
Dredge up the Banquos of past affairs,
And poison each other with the past.

Scene 3

They assassinate each other's friends and families
Until the kitchen is a Malfian charnel house
And no one walks unscathed.

INTERMISSION

The children return from school
And are pushed out to play.

ACT TWO

Scene 1

They each usurp the right to Truth, and visions clash.
Fear reeks in the kitchen
And Anger stalks the breakfast-bar on stilts
Of Righteousness.

Scene 2

Envy and Jealousy present themselves at court
Bringing with them their friends Ridicule and Jibe.

Scene 3

Exhausted they stare at the bending kitchen walls,
At a world convulsed with passion.

Scene 4

Silence.
And a child with a cut knee stands
Weeping at the door,
Face burning in the furnace of this fearful, terrible quiet.

Curtain Down.

Row Two: No-Man's Kitchen

He sulked for days,
Staring at the suddenly strange
Things in the kitchen. The microwave,
The coffee jug, and the kitchen range

All looked different, though they'd not changed.
Was it a trick of the light
That made them look somehow not right?
He wondered was he becoming deranged.

Static crackled in the airwaves,
He smelt the ozone, things were charged.
He felt light, breathless, swollen; large
Swallows of air still left him dazed.

He found himself half-turning in the night,
Forgetting what he'd started to do. Caged
By fences he'd put up himself, the sight
Of her could put him in a rage.

She, frightened—not understanding why
He suddenly stared at her so blindly and cursed—
Hands shaking, unpacked the shopping, and tried
To work out why the kitchen didn't look like hers.

Row Three: War Crimes

For days the house shuddered
To the slamming of doors,
Awash with a silence so thick it could have been riven
With an axe. Chores

Were carried out, robotic;
Meals dropped firmly on the table
Left uneaten, to end up on the fireback. Hypnotic,
The silence became a thing apart, orthogenitic. Unable

To unravel it, it became a border on the map.
They faced across it, sparred, almost broke
Silence to curse, but couldn't snap
The spell. Force fields girdled them. Her mother came, they spoke

As though nothing at all was going on.
'There's a funny smell in here', she said,
Trying to put her finger on the wrong
She felt. She smelt hatred and crueltly. In bed

Their spines touched once or twice:
Electric, ice. She cried silently a few times.
Suddenly he turned and clung to her in the night.
Crossing the border they wiped out all their crimes.

Landfall

Oh we made landfall right enough,
Outriggers out to greet us, singing
Welcomes, nuzzling up against our hull,
Full of fuzzy wuzzies
With flower necklets for us to wear
And orchids for our hair.
                    McDonagh
Was the first over the side,
Head down, falling into the bottle-green
Water, clear as gin, and sinking to
The coral like a mannikin
Tumbling through time.

Surfacing, he swam ashore.
We followed in the boats to where
A sickle bay held cabins and
A spring, some women and a cloud
Of piccaninns.
                    They gave us fruit,
Yams, and sucking pig cooked in
Thick leaves on red-hot rocks.
We gave them pictures of the Queen,
A gun, three bibles, and the pox.

Salalah 1973

The sky's indigo meets the djebel's black,
Confusing the eye into the creation of forms
That do not exist, that have never existed.
There is such light upon the desert
That would have conjured for a hermit, devils on the djebel,
A moonless night and stars strangely muted.

Sudden lines of tracer rule the plain and
Chrysanthemums of mortar shells bloom
In remote pain and die, the wail
Of their growing now filling the dark:
Thunder out of a cloudless sky.
There is no answering fire.

In the morning, the corpses are those
Of a camel train and its driver.
'Sonar picked up a camel fart'
Says a sergeant,
Spooning coconut on his curry,
And the captain, quite jolly,
Said, 'It's often like that
When one's zapping gollies'.

Empty Quarter

From the rim it is a void
So cocksure that the mind spills
Over, reeling with it. Alloyed
To infinity the horizon bends and wavers, fills

And runs, quicksilver, shifting.
The sun batters lizards as
They scatter for cover. Drifting
Dust-devils spool the sand, fast

Fists making the air suddenly solid, mopping
and mowing, creed-mocking;
Behemoth and Beelzebub snickering in the heretic haze
That takes the world and glazes

It, offering the tempter's vision. In this
World nothing holds; sky bends, rock dances,
The desert flexes and the dunes hiss—
Giving no chances.

A body out there dessicates; the wind
Sucks out the juices leaving staring husks to eye
The shaking line that binds
Shuddering earth to viscous sky.

This shriving fire rams cant
Out of you like a punched-out breath,
Leaves you dizzy in the scant
Air shaking on the scorching edge.

Here the flux of philosophy melts.
A line of stones, dry waddis, the sands roll
Towards a low djebel and a belt
Of dunes. Search in the hermit hollow of your soul:

You see a burning plain, no water,
A nomad lost in the empty quarter.

Pharaoh and the Worm

Lord of Lower and Upper Egypt,
Lord of the Nile,
Lord of the World,
Keeper of the Keys of the Gates
Of Abydos through which the souls of all the dead
File down into the underworld.
Lord of all Life, Face of the Sun,
God of the Heavens, Scorpion God,
Amon Ra whose blood flies through
The heavens like the falling stars.

He lies: a cleft stick on his leg
Turns slowly, squeak by squeak,
As inch by inch,
Like the last curlings of the Nile
Through the yellow delta flats,
Like the turnings of gold wire
About the Pharaoh's neck,
Like the spiral of the rays
Circling the sun, the doctor twirls,
Inch by inch, the yard-long guinea worm
From its proud lodging in the Boy-God's thigh.

Al Oud

After they uprooted Saeed's tongue
From the screaming garden of his mouth
And left it flapping on the midden heap,
The Sultan smiling on silk cushions,
Cooled by the marble fountain and its pool, said
'Now poet, sing! Absurd bard, the bird
On the far window ledge sings loud
While you are quiet as the stars, dumb as the sand.'

And Saeed took his knife and from a tree
Fashioned a bird with breast to cradle
And a neck to clasp,
With veins to finger, and a heart
And throat to stroke.
And plucking softly at the strings
He strummed a chord that echoed through
The courtyard like the calls
Of knowing birds, like the shining singing of the stars,
And echoed and re-echoed until it shook the palace walls.